I0019752

Web Application Security is a Stack

How to CYA (Cover Your Apps) Completely

Web Application Security is a Stack

How to CYA (Cover Your Apps) Completely

Lori Mac Vittie

IT Governance Publishing

Every possible effort has been made to ensure that the information contained in this book is accurate at the time of going to press, and the publisher and the author cannot accept responsibility for any errors or omissions, however caused. Any opinions expressed in this book are those of the author, not the publisher. Websites identified are for reference only, not endorsement, and any website visits are at the reader's own risk. No responsibility for loss or damage occasioned to any person acting, or refraining from action, as a result of the material in this publication can be accepted by the publisher or the author.

Apart from any fair dealing for the purposes of research or private study, or criticism or review, as permitted under the Copyright, Designs and Patents Act 1988, this publication may only be reproduced, stored or transmitted, in any form, or by any means, with the prior permission in writing of the publisher or, in the case of reprographic reproduction, in accordance with the terms of licenses issued by the Copyright Licensing Agency. Enquiries concerning reproduction outside those terms should be sent to the publishers at the following address:

IT Governance Publishing
IT Governance Limited
Unit 3, Clive Court
Bartholomew's Walk
Cambridgeshire Business Park
Ely, Cambridgeshire
CB7 4EA
United Kingdom
www.itgovernance.co.uk

© Lori Mac Vittie 2015

The author has asserted the rights of the author under the Copyright, Designs, and Patents Act, 1988, to be identified as the author of this work.

First published in the United Kingdom in 2015
by IT Governance Publishing

ISBN: 978-1-84928-704-3

ABOUT THE AUTHOR

Lori Mac Vittie is responsible for education and evangelism of application services available across F5's entire product suite. Her role includes authorship of technical materials and participation in a number of community-based forums and industry standards organisations, among other efforts. She currently focuses on Cloud computing, infrastructure, DevOps, data centre architecture and security-related topics. Lori has extensive development and technical architecture experience in both high-tech and enterprise organisations, in addition to network and systems administration expertise. Prior to joining F5, Lori was an award-winning technology editor at *Network Computing* magazine.

She holds a BS in Information and Computing Science from the University of Wisconsin at Green Bay, and an MS in Computer Science from Nova Southeastern University. She is technical editor and a member of the steering committee for CloudNOW, a non-profit consortium of the leading women in Cloud computing.

ACKNOWLEDGEMENTS

I would like to thank Antonio Velasco, CEO of Sinersys Technologies, and Giuseppe G. Zorzino CISA CGEIT CRISC, security architect, for their useful contributions during the review process.

CONTENTS

CHAPTER 1: INTRODUCTION

The modern threat

In 2011 an exploit taking advantage of a vulnerability in the Apache web server rapidly circulated across the Internet. Apache, at the time, was used by more than 65% of websites, according to Netcraft, so this was a serious issue which required immediate remediation. The exploit took advantage of a little-known vulnerability in the way Apache handled two HTTP headers. Exploitation of this vulnerability resulted in, as described by CVE-2011-3192, "very significant memory and CPU usage on the server", resulting in a distributed denial-of-service attack (DDoS) through resource exhaustion.

In late 2013, a highly complex DDoS attack[1] on a prominent member of an online trading community was detected and mitigated. In addition to the overwhelming network traffic generated, post-mortem analysis discovered a significant amount of application layer traffic. What had originally appeared to be simply an unusual spike in human interaction was, in truth, driven by a network of nearly 20,000 compromised browsers, all infected with a variant of the PushDo malware.

In early 2014, another vulnerability would shake the foundations of the Internet. Within the implementation of SSL as supported by the open source library, OpenSSL,

---

[1] Application-layer DDoS attacks are becoming increasingly sophisticated, PC World, Oct 2013
http://www.pcworld.com/article/2056805/applicationlayer-ddos-attacks-are-becoming-increasingly-sophisticated.html.

existed the potential for attacks to exploit a buffer-overflow, enabling the extraction of sensitive consumer and corporate data. The open source library was widely used by web servers, as well as a wide variety of open and closed software and hardware around the world. Its discovery led to disruption of business and consumer fears regarding just what data attackers may have been able to extract.

None of these very serious web application vulnerabilities fall under what is traditionally considered the domain of application developers. The term 'web application security' usually conjures up thoughts of the more well-known web application attack vectors, such as SQL injection and cross-site scripting. But the reality is that web application security is not just about the application, but about the 'Web' too. Exploitation of web application platform and protocol implementation is becoming more common and, ultimately, is far more likely to produce the result desired by attackers.

These results are not always the theft of data, as is traditionally put forth. The rise of hacktivism – attacking organisations through their web presence as a means of protest against some business practice or to highlight a social cause – has resulted in a dramatic increase in attacks intended not to steal data or information but to disrupt business operations. These denial-of-service (DoS) attacks generate a lot of press, in addition to the financial costs incurred while applications are unavailable, not to mention the costs to remediate.

Also on the rise are attempts to use vulnerabilities in applications as a delivery vehicle for malware and remote access. Attackers seek not to attack applications themselves, but rather its consumers. By using vulnerabilities in the application layer, attackers can plant, and subsequently deliver, malware and malicious code to a much larger set of victims, some of whom are certain to be compromised and deliver to attackers the resources, data or credentials they are seeking.

The WhiteHat 'Website Security Statistics Report' from May 2013 notes that "23% of organisations website(s) said they experienced a data or system breach as a result of an application layer vulnerability"[2]. An HP TippingPoint sponsored security survey[3] noted that "nearly three in five IT professionals are concerned with application DDoS".

Much of the blame for successful attacks against web applications is laid solely at the feet of the developers who design and build the applications. While many of the attacks rely on common mistakes made during development, it is increasingly the case that attackers are targeting other areas of the web application stack, namely protocols and platforms. Recognising that 'application' security is really a stack, ensures that a growing vector of attacks does not go ignored. Protocol and metadata manipulation attacks are a dangerous source of DDoS and other disruptive techniques that can interrupt business and have a serious impact on the business' bottom line, as well as its reputation.

---

[2] Website Security Statistics Report, May 2013
www.whitehatsec.com/assets/WPstatsReport_052013.pdf.
[3] *http://h30499.www3.hp.com/t5/HP-Security-Products-Blog/TippingPoint-network-security-survey-reveals-top-network/ba-p/6587710#.VAceWvmwLYg.*

A holistic web application security strategy must therefore necessarily view its attack surface as the entire web application stack.

CYA: Cover Your Apps

Web application security must evolve along with the threat spectrum, to ensure complete coverage. Therefore, we will look not only at traditional application logic and data related security issues, but also at protocol and platform concerns. As emerging technologies and architectures, such as Cloud Computing and SDN (Software Defined Networking) continue to advance, application developers are increasingly responsible not only for ensuring compliance with best practices regarding web applications security, but in defining and managing the application policies and procedures that ensure application security at the platform and protocol layers.

Conversely, operators in other organisations are being forced to become more intimately familiar with web applications, in order to implement continuous deployment and delivery in response to pressures to move applications to market faster. Operators must therefore understand the attack vectors against which they must protect those applications, and the various methods which can be used to effectively combat successful exploitation.

With this in mind, this book is intended for application developers, system administrators and operators, as well as networking professionals who need a comprehensive top level view of web application security in order to better defend and protect both the 'Web' and the 'application' against potential attacks. It is not intended to be all encompassing but rather a look at the most common, fundamental attack vectors and defence techniques used to combat such attacks.

CHAPTER 2: ATTACK SURFACE

Web application security tends to be viewed as the purview of developers. It is, after all, about the application, and thus much of the focus on protecting against attacks falls to application developers. The OWASP Top 10, for example, focuses primarily on the methods used by attackers to manipulate application data to gain system access, execute remote commands and generally extract data beyond security controls that may be in place. These attacks target the data exchanged between a client and the application, taking advantage of vulnerabilities in parsing and lax security practices in input validation.

But a web application can also be exploited in other ways. The very logic encoded in an application may be vulnerable. URI or path traversal attacks attempt to exploit a lack of security to access files not intended to be accessed.

These types of attacks are made possible due to assumptions made as to the flow of logic through an application, as well as the methods used to maintain the current state of a web application. The use of cookies as a means to track user location within a workflow, has led to exploitation, as it is rarely the case that such mechanisms are protected against tampering while residing on the client in the browser.

In recent years it has also become commonplace for attackers to target the web application platform and protocols prevalent today. In 2011 a widespread attack on

Apache, known as 'Apache Killer', took advantage of poor handling of an HTTP header in the ubiquitous web server platform to affect a denial of service attack against organisations relying on the web server. As the web server served more than 65% of the sites on the Internet at the time, as tracked by Netcraft[4], the vulnerability rapidly gained the attention of the entire security community.

The result is that the modern web application attack surface should be viewed as a stack, comprising both protocol and more application-specific categories of potential attack surfaces. It is not enough to simply tighten input validation, or apply system-level security to files that should remain inaccessible. The entire stack must be secured against potential attack, lest it be exploited by attackers.

The web application security stack

Those concerned with web application security – whether operators or developers – must view the application layer as comprising its own 'stack', and apply security strategies appropriately.

There are two primary attack surfaces for modern web applications: the web application itself and the platform upon which it is deployed. The two are inseparable; you cannot deploy a web application without a platform on which it can run. Apache, NGINX, IBM WebSphere and Microsoft IIS are among the most popular platforms upon which web applications are deployed. Attacks on web

---

[4]   *http://news.netcraft.com/archives/2011/07/08/july-2011-web-server-survey.html*.

applications, as well as their underlying platforms, are common, and the reliance of web applications on the platform to provide data regarding state, and other relevant information, introduces additional risk.

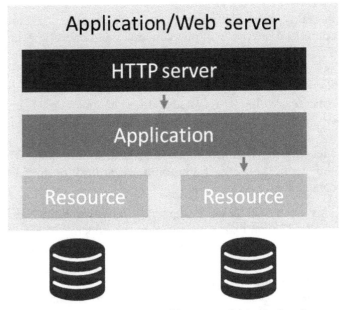

Figure 1: High-level architecture of a typical web application

It is important to make a distinction between the *platform* and the *application* because of the impact it has on security. As depicted in *Figure 1*, most web applications rely on an HTTP server embedded in the web application platform. The HTTP server ensures compliance with the

HTTP protocol, by ensuring that all web servers implement HTTP in the same way. While there are certainly deviations where the HTTP specification does not prescribe specific behaviour, for the most part, interoperability between any two components which speak HTTP is assured by the meticulous attention to supporting the HTTP protocol as specified.

In reality, most platforms are far more complex; they are comprised internally of many modules and micro-systems that provide for a variety of web application needs, such as messaging, queuing, standards support, identity services and more. While there may certainly be security concerns with these systems, from an operational and development perspective the most relevant distinction is the separation of the HTTP server from the application execution environment. This is consistent across all web and application server platforms, regardless of internal complexity or design.

This general design supports interoperability and standardisation that is beneficial to developers and has, in fact, been a significant driver of web growth through the years; it also has the effect of isolating core HTTP behaviour and data from developers. Web developers do not have access to the parsing routines, for example, that are contained within the HTTP servers themselves. The HTTP server is, essentially, a black box which sits between the user and the application.

This is the reason a vulnerability within a platform is incredibly dangerous, especially if that platform is widely deployed. As a 'black box', only the provider of the platform can offer a patch to address a vulnerability which may leave applications and organisations at risk. This was the case with Apache Killer. The vulnerability lay within the HTTP server component in the protocol parsing logic. While Apache is open source and any organisation could have theoretically patched the vulnerability by modifying the code directly, the practicality of doing so meant the only viable response was to wait for a patch to be issued.

This is not meant to pick on Apache. Many other platforms have also suffered similar vulnerabilities but most have not received the same level of attention, mostly due to Apache's dominance of the market at the time.

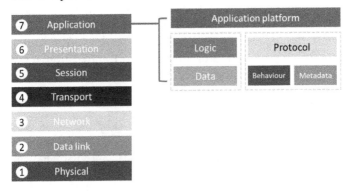

Figure 2: The modern attack surface includes application logic and protocols

This interdependence between platform and application necessarily means that web application security must be attentive to both platform vulnerabilities – usually related to protocols – and the application itself.

From this we derive the web application security 'stack'; a combination of concerns comprising both the platform protocol support and the web application. Each of these stacks is further distinguished by attack surfaces specific to behaviour or metadata on the protocol side, and by logic and data on the web application side.

To comprehensively secure a web application against the myriad of modern, attack vectors threatening them, it is necessary to understand both stacks from the perspective of their unique threat vectors.

Application: Platform

Just about every application is deployed on some kind of platform: Apache, IIS, IBM WebSphere, etc. The list goes on and on. It is important to remember the existence of the platform and the role it plays for applications. Application platforms provide the protocol support applications need to communicate over a network. TCP, and to a large extent, HTTP, are all handled within the framework of an application platform. Developers rarely interact at the transport (usually TCP) layer, and largely only deal with the application (HTTP) layer from a content exchange perspective, thus it is easy to forget that they may be vulnerable to exploitation and attack.

There are two distinct layers of the network stack that include protocols ripe for web application attacks in the application platform: transport and application.

Transport protocols
The first of these is the transport layer, commonly referred to as layer 4, due to its location in the traditional OSI network model. Web applications use TCP as their transport protocol because of its reliable nature. That is, delivery of the packets making up a conversation between

client and server are carefully monitored for delivery, with error recovery mechanisms built into the protocol.

These mechanisms can, and are, exploited to attack web applications. The most common attack at this protocol layer is a SYN flood. This attack abuses TCP by taking advantage of session timeout values to establish idle sessions, until the server runs out of resources and can no longer respond to additional requests.

This type of attack can only be mitigated in flight or by the web platform itself; the developer has no control over the behaviour of TCP and has no simple way to evaluate behaviour indicative of such an attack. Such attacks are best mitigated by upstream infrastructure, such as the load balancer, web application firewall, or stateful data centre firewall, as they are able to both detect, and reject, such attacks.

Operators and administrators can consider changes to web platform configuration directives which impact TCP idle and timeout behaviour, but these can negatively impact valid web application behaviour and thus the decision to do so should be undertaken cautiously and with full understanding of the impact on other applications and consumers.

Secure transport protocols
In the OSI network model, application transport security protocols, such as SSL and TLS, are often found at layer 5, but they are sometimes lumped in with layer 4 and other times with layer 7.

While there are good arguments to be had by everyone on this topic, the important thing to note is that both SSL and

TLS are designed to provide transport layer security, and both are potential threat vectors. Recent web application attacks have leveraged vulnerabilities in SSL (Heartbleed, 2014), as well as TLS (man-in-the-middle renegotiation attack, 2009).

These attacks – like those targeting TCP – are the responsibility of the web platform. Unlike those targeting TCP, there is very little the operator or administrator can do to mitigate such vulnerabilities when they are discovered. Approaches to resolution include simply shutting down (not recommended) or leveraging upstream infrastructure capabilities to detect and mitigate.

More dangerous than the exploitation of vulnerabilities in secure protocol implementations, however, is the false sense of security often associated with the use of SSL and TLS. SSL and TLS are transport layer security mechanisms designed purely to prevent data in flight from being modified, or seen, by someone other than the intended receiver. Data is encrypted to prevent others from seeing or modifying the data, but it does not guarantee that the data itself is safe. Malicious code, or content that is encrypted, is still malicious code or content. Encryption can actually have the effect of obscuring a web application attack, by preventing security infrastructure and web platform protection mechanisms from being able to inspect the content.

Web application protocols
Finally, we reach the highest layer of the OSI network model – layer 7 – at which the application resides. This is where HTTP lives and where most web application attacks occur.

HTTP, unlike most other protocols, crosses the line between a network protocol which handles communication between a client and the server, and an application protocol which carries with it data relevant to the behaviour of an application.

HTTP can be broken down into two distinct protocol layers: metadata and behaviour.

HTTP metadata

HTTP headers contain metadata which is important to both the platform and the web application. Many of these headers are well known and understood, for example:

- Cookie
- User agent
- Host
- Content-length
- Content-type
- Accept
- Status
- Connection
- Server.

Some HTTP headers are included only on request, others only on response.

HTTP metadata is generally accessible within the web application, which results in another attack surface, but in terms of the platform, the risk is platform layer vulnerabilities in the handling (parsing) of these pieces of data.

The primitive data type for variable data shared via HTTP headers is ultimately a string, and string data types are vulnerable to a variety of attack methods due to lapses in secure coding practices. Buffer overflows, or variables that are evaluated and executed at the system level, are examples of such potential attack vectors.

HTTP behaviour

HTTP behaviour describes the interaction at the protocol level between the client and the server. There is a well-defined flow of how messages should be exchanged between an HTTP client (such as a browser) and the server. Behavioural vulnerabilities can be detected by recognising when behaviour is anomalous, based on standardised interactions.

While not a perfect indicator of an attack, odd interactions can indicate an impending or executing attack.

The problem here is that the application platforms generally have no built-in ability to recognise anomalous behaviour. Furthermore, it is generally the case that web servers are topologically deployed behind a series of other network devices, making it impossible for the platform to have knowledge of information relevant to interpreting the behaviour of the client within context.

For example, the network over which a client accesses a web application is relevant when detecting resource consumption-based denial-of-service attacks. The client purposefully accepts data at a rate slower than their network indicates they are capable of, in an attempt to maintain an open connection as long as possible. The result is that the web server's send queue remains filled, which consumes additional memory resources. If enough clients are engaged in this attack, the server can become overwhelmed with the number of open connections and data waiting in the send queue, and become unresponsive.

Unfortunately, web application platforms are not enabled with the ability to detect these attacks, nor are they topologically in the right location necessary to deduce the client's appropriate network speed, even if they were.

Application: Logic

Application logic is defined as the expected steps a user takes while interacting with the application. For example, it is expected that the first step for any user is to log-in to the application. Then, depending on the purpose of the application, the user might typically navigate to one of a set of business functions, and subsequently navigate through a business process encapsulated by the application.

In addition to the navigation through a business process within an application, application logic comprises discrete processing steps. There is (or should be) a defined set of steps that must be taken to get from point A to point Z. Deviation from that path is often considered a behavioural anomaly. It is these deviations that often cause faults in the application that result in escalation of privileges, or access to information that would otherwise be denied.

The sheer complexity of web applications, and the business processes encapsulated by them, means testing often fails to evaluate security in terms of outlying behavioural patterns. Tests are designed specifically to evaluate the correctness of the flow, as designated by the business process. Only when a user inexperienced with the process begins to seemingly randomly 'click around' in the application do these vulnerable flows become apparent.

Such vulnerabilities are generally present due to assumptions made by the developer about the flow. For example, a user will already be logged in when they click on 'retrieve customer data', therefore there is no reason to validate credentials.

Another common application logic vulnerability is reliance on role-based filtering in the application to prevent access to data. This is due to the assumption that the user will only use the user interface to navigate the application. Attackers can often manipulate the URL directly to bypass restrictions imposed by the GUI, on the assumption that the developer has assumed the GUI will enforce the application logic necessary to prevent access to unauthorised data or business functions.

Applications also commonly enforce application or business logic flow through the use of 'hidden' parameters or cookies. Attackers adept at reverse engineering can inject new values into these parameters and cookies that violate business logic, based on either established process, or limitations based on role or subscription level of the user. Because the hidden parameters and cookies are trusted by the developer as being authoritative, manipulating these values can easily bypass logic and enable exploitation to the attacker's advantage.

The increasing use of JavaScript on the client to enforce business logic requiring is also problematic because of the ease with which such logic can be made visible to attackers. It is increasingly common for sites to use CSS overlays, for example, to force a user to log-in to a site. Integrated developer tools within browsers allow easy access to the DOM and, in turn, enable attackers to modify, and even delete, elements and scripts governing data input. This leaves the application open to exploitation.

Other abuses of application logic can include denying service to a user by intentionally locking them out of their account. As most web applications today have controls that disallow 'too many' attempts to log-in, it is a simple thing to exceed the log-in attempt limit and subsequently 'lock out' an account.

These kinds of logical vulnerabilities are difficult to find, precisely because they often do not follow any specific pattern. Random navigation and manipulation of URLs is not generally part of the unit testing performed by developers, and is difficult to codify. In environments increasingly driven by test automation, both for functional completeness and security, the randomness associated with vulnerabilities in application logic are difficult to codify and test, leaving applications vulnerable, unless targeted, secure coding practices are applied during development.

Application: Data

If there was an attack surface that springs to mind when the words 'application security' are mentioned, it is application data. The attack surface presented by application data is spread very wide, comprising everything from input to output and processing itself.

Securing application data is made more difficult in web applications due to the interconnected nature of such applications. Content and even processing, can, and often, does rely on external applications. This reliance necessarily introduces additional attack surfaces that are particularly troubling because they are not under the control of the developer. Additional care must be taken with the inclusion of external applications in web applications to compensate for potential vulnerabilities that may pose a threat.

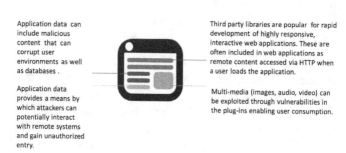

Application data can include malicious content that can corrupt user environments as well as databases .

Application data provides a means by which attackers can potentially interact with remote systems and gain unauthorized entry.

Third party libraries are popular for rapid development of highly responsive, interactive web applications. These are often included in web applications as remote content accessed via HTTP when a user loads the application.

Multi-media (images, audio, video) can be exploited through vulnerabilities in the plug-ins enabling user consumption.

Figure 3: Web application data introduces multiple attack surfaces

Web application data is considered unstructured; that is there is no specification which governs the format of the data. While web applications are often composed of a variety of structured data that are governed by specifications, such as XML, JSON, HTML and CSS, modern web applications also include a variety of less-structured and unstructured data, such as JavaScript, audio and video data, documents, as well as images.

Because of the reliance of plug-ins to display many types of unstructured data, the attack surface of a web application also extends to the plug-ins that may be required for users to consume such data. Vulnerabilities in plug-ins – particularly widely used ones, such as Adobe for PDF – have been effectively exploited in the past to infect client devices with malware intended for various nefarious purposes.

Similarly, the application data is what ends up stored in, and acted upon, by a database – whether relational or not. That leaves databases and systems that rely on data to communicate with other systems, vulnerable to attacks, due to manipulation of those systems through the data. This is how SQL injection attacks are carried out – hiding within the data, masquerading as valid characters that, when interpreted by a database, will yield a variety of disastrous results, including data leakage, corruption of the database and introduction of malicious content.

Web application data provides the broadest attack surface in the web application security stack, making it the most difficult to secure against exploitation.

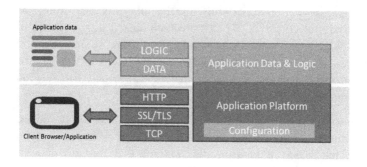

Figure 4: Attack surface relationships between client and application

CHAPTER 3: THREAT VECTORS

As we have seen, there are a wide variety of ways in which attackers can exploit web applications. Many of the available attack surfaces provide miscreants with the ability to carry out several different types of attacks. Attackers, it turns out, are not all motivated by the same end goals. Some attack for profit, others for fun, others for revenge, and some are in the business of collecting end-user systems that can later be rented out to attackers for nefarious purposes.

The end goal of the attackers – the human part of the equation – is outside the scope of this book. The technical reasons for attacks will be the focus of this chapter.

There are three distinct threat vectors for applications upon which attackers are focused:

1. Data
2. Protocols
3. Availability.

Threat vector: Data

In December 2013 we learned of an attack on the retail store, Target, in which attackers were successfully able to infiltrate, and gather, the personal information of an estimated 70 million consumers, as well as the more sensitive financial information (credit and debit card data) from as many as 40 million customers. Just over six months later, a Russian 'gang' notified the world that it had managed to pull off the theft of over 1.2 billion email addresses. Addresses which will be used for a variety of purposes, including SPAM operations.

The news is riddled with stories of attacks yielding increasingly larger pay outs in terms of data. More disturbing is the frequency with which these occur and the overall customer impact, both of which are also increasing.

Data is a tempting target for attackers. While it is important to draw a line between corporate and personal data, it is most often the case that attackers seek access to the latter, by targeting the former. As applications have evolved, and organisations realise that online applications are able to divulge much more information about customers and potential customers than their brick and mortar counterparts, organisations have sought to collect it both directly and indirectly. That personal data has become part of an integral piece of corporate data, nowadays referred to as 'big data', and is treated similarly to any other customer data that might be stored by the collecting organisation.

Exfiltration

The data most often sought for collection – personally identifiable information (PII) – is highly prized for its value on the information black market, as it can be used to perpetrate identity fraud, as well as for executing automated financial transactions.

Even email addresses are valuable today, as organisations use them in a similar way to other pieces of PII for identification. More dangerous, perhaps, is the use of email addresses as part of the authentication and credential recovery process. Attackers gaining access to a customer's email account have managed to obtain the keys to the kingdom, as it were.

While there are certainly attackers who seek more company-focused data, corporate espionage has always been more successful as a topic for movies and books than a significant driver of information security practices. Personal data is just too lucrative a business (and make no mistake it is a business, albeit a shady one) to ignore.

Data-based attacks, therefore, generally focus on the gathering of data suitable for sale or personal use.

A sample of data-based attacks:

- Web scraping is the process of collecting information from websites, typically using automated programs, or bots (short for web robots).
- Session hijacking. Web servers often send session tokens to the client browser upon successful client authentication. A session token is usually a string of variable width, and it could be placed in the URL, in the header of an HTTP request as a cookie, in other parts of the header of an HTTP request, or in the body of the HTTP request. Session hijacking compromises the session token by stealing, or predicting, a valid session token to gain unauthorised access to the web server.
- Parameter tampering. Attacks involve the manipulation of parameters exchanged between client and server to modify application data, such as user credentials and permissions, or the price and quantity of products.

Attackers use a variety of techniques with which to obtain the data they desire. Since the advent of the Internet era, in which connectivity is almost always assured, attackers have learned to harness the power of billions of connected devices to aid them in their quest to identity targets and collect data through mass attacks. These attacks are generally relatively simple and focus on preventable coding errors in the queries made from a web application to a corporate data source.

There are two ways in which attackers attempt to infiltrate transactions as a means to collect data: through the server and through the client. Both use a technique called 'injection' but target different aspects of the application.

Injection – Server exploitation

By manipulating the input data, which is almost always used to create a database query, attackers can use lax input validation to ensure an attack successfully penetrates into the data tier and yields results.

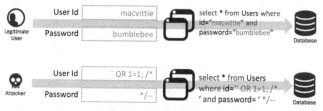

Figure 5: An SQL injection attack is easy to perpetrate when little or no checks are placed on user provided input

It is not only user input that poses a risk for data exfiltration attacks. In the spring of 2014, a vulnerability in the OpenSSL library used to support encryption (SSL and TLS) protocols resulted in a significant exfiltration attack. It is estimated that some half a million websites and applications were vulnerable to the subsequently named 'Heartbleed' attack. The attack used a buffer overflow vulnerability in the security protocols to obtain data that was otherwise thought to be secure. Personal information, as well as cryptographic certificates and keys were obtained, and sent most of the Internet into a tizzy. Even though the odds of successfully using Heartbleed to obtain specific personal or corporate data were minimal, the ubiquitous connectivity of the Internet, combined with the ability to automate attacks, improved the odds considerably.

Injection – Client exploitation

Injection on the client is similar to other exfiltration attack methods, such as SQL injection but is not intended to gather large amounts of data. Rather, script injection seeks to insert capabilities into the client side logic, by injecting scripts and modifying the DOM that governs the appearance of the page.

The scripts are designed to do a variety of things, including capturing and modifying data, without alerting the victim to their presence. These attacks are commonly referred to as man-in-the-browser (MITB) attacks. The MITB attack is more authentic than phishing attacks that rely on cloned websites that purport to be a victim's trusted site, as there are rarely any visual clues in the URL or host name, or in the make up of the site itself. Increasingly these attacks target online banking web applications. The initial entry point onto the client system is generally through an add-on to the browser or via malware unknowingly deposited on the client machine. The malware component allows attackers to inject scripts into web pages that enable a variety of attack surfaces, including remote control of the machine through VNC or RDP.

The scripts injected into the web application are able to extract and capture data, such as credentials, as well as take advantage of client-side capabilities to connect to other systems and deposit the stolen information for later use.

These MITB attacks are increasingly problematic; in 2013, 41% of organisations suffering from fraud implicated a Trojan (Neverquest, Zeus, Cridex) that directly used this attack surface to carry out banking fraud[5].

Infection

The victim's machine is infected with the Trojan

Injection

The infected victim visits the banking site.

HOW MITB WORKS

Malicious script intercepts credentials, stores and delivers them to the dropzone.

The victim logs in to the site

Figure 6: MITB attacks begin with an infection and use script injection to steal data from victims

---

[5] ISMG 2013 Faces of Fraud Survey.

Exfiltration attacks look for weaknesses in applications and protocols that will yield attackers a significant amount of data, or highly valuable data. Unfortunately for security professionals and consumers alike, there are almost always weaknesses that can be exploited.

Corruption

A secondary data-based attack is designed not to collect data but rather corrupt it. There are two purposes to corrupting data: plant the seeds for future attacks, or destruction. The former is far more common than the latter, but when corruption is used to destroy data, it is far more devastating to the victim.

Corruption attacks are usually part of larger, more complex schemes that require many discrete systems to interact. Because consumers interact with many different sites and applications, they, and their system resources, are often sought to be used as a distribution channel for malware and other viruses, as well as for directly gathering PII from the victim.

Attackers seek to plant tools within the data that will eventually provide them with the ability to collect personal data, or use the victim's resources for other types of attack. The ultimate target is often credentials, or resources that can be used by attackers to perpetrate fraud, or carry out other attacks against larger, corporate victims.

Data can also be corrupted in the sense that it is changed in ways as to be more favourable to attackers. For example, cookie tampering (or poisoning) takes advantages of the reliance applications have on cookies to maintain state for an application. At issue is the level of trust in the integrity of the cookie which is, after all, just a text value stored within easy reach of the end-user.

Attackers can modify cookies that may control privilege levels, application state, pricing and other consumer information that impacts billing, or transactional values, quite easily. Applications that store critical data as cookies are vulnerable to tampering attacks that may radically impact the security of not only the application but entire systems.

Threat vector: Protocols

Data exfiltration attacks generally require local access to the intended victim's browser. Another avenue of attack, however, is to deposit the instruments of attack remotely, by exploiting both human nature, as well as known vulnerabilities in the application protocols used by all web applications: HTTP.

There are two primary threat vectors that take advantage of HTTP. Both exploit vulnerabilities in the technologies upon which developers rely to compose web applications. In addition to HTML, scripting and style-sheets are commonly used in modern web applications to enable an interactive and more responsive experience. These technologies enhance the capabilities of a web application by allowing them to perform 'hidden' transactions, as well as incorporate remote, third party resources in their application.

Both are just as commonly exploited.

```
<script src="http://yui.yahooapis.com/3.17.2/build/yui/yui-min.js"></script>
```

Cross-site scripting (XSS)

Cross-site scripting (XSS) is an injection-style attack initiated by the loading of a compromised resource from a remote site. Because the resource is loaded from a (purportedly) trusted site, the data and logic it includes are rarely validated or examined for malicious content. In this way, attackers can inject behaviour into a web application that is intended to result in data exfiltration or other fraudulent activities.

These scripts, which may include a variety of web application technologies, such as HTML, CSS, or JavaScript, are included into a web page through the use of HTTP. The script's location may be on a third-party site. For example, the Yahoo IO UI library is available to all developers and can be easily included in any web application using the following code:

Developers may include scripts from a variety of sources. All will use HTTP as the means to locate and transfer the script into the application. Many will obfuscate the actual code and data within the script, and some will further occlude the actual script name to avoid automated scanner detection. These types of evasion techniques are common and succeed at an alarmingly good rate.

Such scripts have access to cookies, session data, or other sensitive information relevant to the site. Some scripts are also able to rewrite content in much the same manner as a MITB attack.

The open web application security project (OWASP) lists XSS among its 'top ten' vulnerabilities[6]. Industry security vendors will eagerly relate the number of XSS vulnerabilities discovered in live web applications, as well as statistics regarding the losses and impact of this vulnerability. It is pervasive, to say the least.

Such attempts can also be combined with injection-style attacks, to force the loading of malicious scripts from external sources. Applications that store string-based data from users can be manipulated into storing a malicious script that, when later rendered in the browser, will trigger the loading of an external script designed to execute a variety of actions, such as keylogging.

These scripts are more often than not obfuscated in such a way as to make them difficult to detect. For example, the script location may be encoded or encrypted using one of the many HTML encoding types. Decimals, hexadecimals and special characters are often used to 'hide' an attack and evade detection.

```
<IMG SRC=&#106;&#97;&#118;&#97;&#115;&#99;&#114;&#105;&#112;&#116;&#58;&#97;&#108;&#101;&#114;
&#116;&#40; &#39;&#88;&#83;&#83;&#39;&#41;>
```

Figure 7: Example of an encoded XSS attack

Cross-site request forgery (CSRF)

CSRF is less often discussed than its XSS cousin, likely owing to better security models that are able to prevent a

---

[6] *www.owasp.org/index.php/Top_10_2013-Top_10*.

significant portion of such attacks, as well as the greater difficulty in carrying one out.

CSRF relies on two separate interactions and generally requires social engineering and careful timing to pull off, as it relies on the user being logged into one site while simultaneously opening some malicious content in another. Attacks have used web-based email, as well as injection, to carry out CSRF attacks, and they are still listed as one of the more common vulnerabilities in most annual reports that track security topics.

CSRF works by using the identity and privileges of the victim as identified by an existing, authenticated session. Basically, it exploits the trust relationship between an authenticated user and the site, to execute illicit transactions. For example, if you are logged into your banking site and open a connection to a second site that contains a CSRF exploit, the second site can essentially hijack your credentials and information from the existing session with the banking site and perform transactions out of sight. Generally, these attacks take advantage of the XMLHttpRequest object that rose to popular usage during the explosion of Web 2.0 sites and AJAX-based applications. This browser object allows 'hidden' transactions to be performed using JavaScript, without any interaction, or even knowledge, by the user.

This attack, like XSS, relies on scripting embedded in a web page. This means the attack can be contained within any HTML element in a page, including images and other assumed binary content elements, as well as the commonly exploited iframe element.

```
<iframe src="http://mybank.com/app/transfer?srcAcct=10100100101&amount=1500&dstAcct=... >
```

Figure 8: A typical CSRF attack to execute a financial transaction

Though the biggest concern is often to protect against CSRF for financial purposes, it is important to note that attackers can, and do, leverage CSRF to gain access to networks and systems as a first step in a much more complex attack scheme.

For example, it can be assumed that if an operator is reading a manual about a router, or other network equipment, that they are probably also logged into the administrative interface for that device. As these interfaces are often web-based today, a CSRF attack could be used to modify the configuration of that device and thus change its behaviour. One might attempt to allow access from an external IP address for later exploitation, or simply redirect routing, such that a DDoS is effectively executed.

```
<img src="http://192.168.1.1/admin/config/access?allow=10.10.1.89" height="1" width="1"/>
```

Figure 9: A CSRF attack modifying a network device configuration might be implanted in the online manual

No matter the purpose behind the attack, suffice to say that it requires more coordination than other web application attacks, but when successfully executed can yield significant results.

Like most attacks, there have been noteworthy exploits using the technique. In 2011, an SSL/TLS exploit, known as BEAST (Browser Exploit Against SSL/TLS), made the rounds. BEAST was a combination of a man-in-the-middle and CSRF attack that resulted in the theft of protected data stored in encrypted cookies, such as log-in or account information exchanged with sites through which payments and other privacy-sensitive transactions are made.

While XSS and CSRF are the most common HTTP-based attacks, largely due to the ease of implementation, they are not the only application protocol level attacks. Some attacks take advantage of HTTP behaviour and handling in proxy systems, to carry out an attack against the web application (through an HTTP request), or against a user (through the HTTP response).

HTTP request smuggling

HTTP request smuggling relies on the existence of intermediary systems, such as proxies and load balancers that parse the HTTP headers in a different way than the web application server. The attackers hide malicious code in the headers, with the expectation it will be delivered to the web application server by the intermediate device.

This technique can be used to poison caches, hijack sessions, or execute XSS. Most importantly, it indicates the ability to bypass an intermediate device, such as a web application firewall.

```
GET /mypage.php?parm1=val1&parm2=

Content-Type: application/x-www-form-

Content-Length: 0
```

```
Foo: GET /mypage.php   HTTP/1.1

Cookie: id=9811991

Authorization: Basic tinargyztldkdppedzzt
```

Figure 10: The 'Foo' header here is an attempt at HTTP request smuggling

Other attempts at request smuggling include duplicating the headers, with the second set containing an attack. This is based on the assumption that when the intermediate system encounters the second set of headers, it will simply use them instead of the first set.

HTTP response splitting

A second HTTP-based attack is response splitting. This attack attempts to deliver malicious data to the user on the response to a legitimate request.

The attack requires the attacker to be able to inject malicious code into the response. This can occur by compromising a service upon which the application relies for data, but is more commonly carried out by injecting the code into an HTTP header on the client side, with the expectation it will be carried through and returned.

Response splitting relies on the HTTP standard method of indicating a new line, namely the use of a carriage return (CR or ASCII 0x0D) and line feed (LF or ASCII 0x0A) combination. By adding these two characters to an HTTP header that is carried through from request to response, such as a cookie might be, the attacker can deliver malicious code. This is often used to split the response, by including a second, complete response (including headers) after the carriage-return line-feed combination. The client sees two responses and parses both. The second, malicious response might contain the link to a script (XSS), or to a malware executable that will be automatically loaded.

HTTP header vulnerabilities

Over the past few years a number of vulnerabilities in HTTP have been discovered lurking in the headers used by the protocol. For example, in 2009 SANS discovered a way to exploit Roundcube Webmail via the HTTP accept header. The attack was actually designed to trick the server into executing a system-level command to extract data not normally accessible to external users.

Figure 11: Example attack via HTTP accept header

What the attackers in this example were attempting to do is trick the application into evaluating system commands encoded in the Accept header, in order to retrieve some data they should not have had access to. The purpose of the attack, however, could easily have been for some other nefarious deed, such as potentially writing a file to the system that could be used as a cross-site scripting attack, or deleting files, or just generally wreaking havoc with the system.

Since then, there have been a number of other vulnerabilities in HTTP headers that have been discovered and exploited. Such vulnerabilities are extremely dangerous because they occur in the web server, which may be deployed across hundreds or thousands (or more) of websites across the Internet.

Heartbleed (2014) was thought to have impacted more than half a million sites across the Internet, thanks to the pervasiveness of the OpenSSL library inclusion in web server platforms.

Threat vector: Availability
In the past few years the term DDoS (distributed denial-of-service) has climbed out of the lower layers of the network stack and into the application layers. Both vendors and analysts have noted an increase in the frequency, and success, of such attacks.

The rise of 'hacktivism' and state-sponsored attacks is partially to blame. Groups, such as Anonymous, are well known for their targeting of specific web applications and sites, based on political or social agendas. Regardless of the motivation behind web application attacks targeting availability, the fact remains that successful attacks do considerable economic and often brand damage to victims.

DDoS attacks against a web application primarily target HTTP. They attempt to exploit the expected behaviour of the protocol to their advantage. They are not exploiting vulnerabilities at all, but rather using the protocols against the organisation in an attempt to consume all available resources, such that legitimate users cannot access them.

Application DDoS attacks are more insidious than their network counterparts because they take advantage of application protocol behaviours, but unlike their network-based counterparts, it requires far fewer clients to overwhelm a host. This is part of the reason application-based DDoS attacks are so hard to detect – because there are fewer clients necessary (owing to the large chunks of resources consumed by a single client) they don't fit the 'blast' pattern that is so typical of a network-based DDoS. It can take literally millions of ICMP requests to saturate a host and its network, but it requires only tens of thousands of requests to consume the resources of an application host such that it becomes unreliable and unavailable. And given the ubiquitous nature of HTTP – over which most of these attacks are perpetrated – and the relative ease with which it is possible to hijack unsuspecting browsers and force their participation in such an attack – an attack can be in progress and look like nothing more than a 'flash crowd' – a perfectly acceptable, and in many industries, desirable event.

A common method of attack involves saturating the target (victim) machine with external communications requests, so that the target system cannot respond to legitimate traffic, or responds so slowly as to be rendered effectively unavailable. In general terms, DDoS attacks are implemented by forcing the targeted computer to reset, or by consuming its resources so that it can no longer provide its intended service, or by obstructing the communication media between the intended users and the victim so that they can no longer communicate adequately.

HTTP GET flood

An HTTP GET flood is as exactly as it sounds: it's a massive influx of legitimate HTTP GET requests that come from large numbers of users, usually connection-oriented bots. These requests mimic legitimate users and are nearly impossible for applications, and even harder for traditional security components, to detect. The result of this attack is similar to the effect: server errors, increasingly degraded performance and resource exhaustion.

This attack is particularly dangerous to applications deployed in Cloud-based environments (public or private) that are enabled with auto-scaling policies, as the system will respond to the attack by launching more and more instances of the application. Limits must be imposed on auto-scaling policies to ensure the financial impact of an HTTP GET flood does not become overwhelming.

Slowloris

Slowloris consumes resources by 'holding' connections open by sending partial HTTP requests. It subsequently sends headers at regular intervals to keep the connections from timing out, or being closed due to lack of activity. This causes resources on the web/application servers to remain dedicated to the clients attacking and keeps them unavailable for fulfilling legitimate requests.

Slow HTTP POST

A slow HTTP POST is a twist on slowloris, in which the client sends POST headers with a legitimate content-length. After the headers are sent, the message body is transmitted at slow speed, thus tying up the connection (server resources) for long periods of time. A relatively small number of clients performing this attack can effectively consume all resources on the web/application server and render it useless to legitimate users.

It is by no means the case that all DDoS attacks take advantage of HTTP. There are plenty of examples of web-based attacks (LOIC, for example) that are initiated in the browser but target the more traditional network stack, using TCP and UDP floods to overwhelm the site. These are important vectors of which to be aware but they are outside the scope of this book, as they are often treated as typical network DDOS attacks and are mitigated by application delivery or network firewalls.

CHAPTER 4: THREAT MITIGATION

Mitigating threats across the web application stack requires consideration of the primary threat vectors through which web applications are attacked. This is made more difficult by the reality that not all attackers are human; attacks are often carried out by compromised devices that have fallen prey to malware. Careful consideration of all interaction with users is necessary, including attempting to distinguish between bots, spiders and human beings.

There are three logical points at which it makes sense to apply application security policies. Each provides the means to apply a different approach to mitigating potential attacks, based on the state of the exchange. Some mitigation techniques are best applied external to the web application platform, others are agnostic with respect to location.

The three logical points at which web application security is best applied are: on connect, on request and on response. Together, these enable a focus on the three Cs of application security: client, context and content.

THE THREE Cs OF APPLICATION SECURITY

CLIENT	CONTEXT	CONTENT
ON CONNECT	ON REQUEST	ON RESPONSE
Evaluate client status, network, location and device before allowing interaction with any application.	Inspect requests, especially those containing user input or cookies. Be careful if extracting data from URIs.	Inspect responses. Scan for sensitive data in payloads. Check for content exceeding normal response sizes.

Figure 12: The three Cs of application security

These basic building blocks promote an approach that evaluates exchanges, both inbound and outbound, and takes into consideration the evolving mobile and Cloud landscape in which clients (both consumers and employees) might be accessing applications from locations external to a corporate controlled network.

The three Cs of application security

Client

When a client connects – or attempts to connect – to an application, it offers the first opportunity to mitigate a pending attack. Inbound requests to connect carry with them certain details that can be inferred from the underlying network protocols. Information, such as IP address (location), client device type and relevant network data (speed), can be used to grant or deny access before an attack can be launched.

On an initial connection, for example, it may be prudent to deny access to clients accessing the application based on location. For example, if the application is one used by employees only and all employees are located in a specific set of geographical regions, it would logically follow that attempts to access that application from outside those established regions might be an attack.

This method of protection relies on geolocation capabilities which are often implemented in the network, outside the web application platform.

Context

The next logical point at which web application security can be applied is on the inbound request. As noted earlier, HTTP headers carry with them a significant amount of detail about the client that can be used to determine the legitimacy of a request. Whether it is agent type – browser, operating system, etc. – or languages and content types they will accept, the HTTP headers of an incoming request are a treasure trove of security-related data that can be used to determine whether to allow, or deny, a given request.

The HTTP headers also contain the URI being requested, along with any cookies related to the application. These values must be critically examined, as both are subject to tampering that can indicate an attempted attack.

A URI is particularly susceptible to being modified as part of a logic based attack that can result in escalated privileges, or avoidance of business logic, that might catch an attack between steps. This type of attack is hard to detect unless there is a known flow of URIs through the application. For example, log-in must occur before modifying a client record, or users must verify client account information before they can access a page that allows modification. The proper logical flow through an application should be enforced to avoid potential attacks that skip steps.

It is important to evaluate requests in the context that they are made; that is, a request to checkout by itself is not necessarily a red flag. If that request immediately follows a log-in with no intervening steps, however, it should be viewed suspiciously, as it deviates from typical application flow.

These types of attacks are also often used to circumvent input validation embedded in the client-side of the application. Many web applications include scripts designed to help users with formatting of data, especially with dates or account numbers. These data input handlers are also able to ensure that extra data, such as often found in SQL injection attacks, cannot be included in the input.

By entering the data as part of the URI, attackers can circumvent the protections built into the application on the client-side.

```
<form action="/search" method=get>
```

```
Search: <input type=text name=search
onChange="javascript:
validateQuery(this.value);">

<input type=submit value=Search>
```

Figure 13: A standard HTTP form identifies the relative URI which will be invoked on submission

In this form, handlers are attached to each of the input fields. Under normal operation, these handlers would force users to only enter data considered valid for the field in question. But by submitting the query by directly crafting a URI, the attacker is able to circumvent the handler's security checks.

```
http://site.com/search?search='something;
select * from users'
```

Figure 14: The attacker directly enters a URI submitting an embedded attack to the server

This is not to say that client-side input validation is a waste of time. It serves to improve productivity and the user experience, in addition to its security aspects, but it is important to note that it can be circumvented and a layered approach may yield better results.

Content

Finally, it is important to examine content in responses. Many attacks might be thwarted if only someone examined the response content and noticed it contained sensitive information, or was significantly larger than it should have been.

The most common implementations of response-based mitigations focus on stripping personal data, such as account or government issued identification numbers from responses. This is a good first step, but the technique can also be used to detect attempts to gather information in general. For example, a successful SQL injection attack rarely attempts to get just one piece of data. They are after lists. Lists are rather lengthy, and it should be obvious to an observer when the content length of a response is too large for the given request.

Similarly, it is important to evaluate the type of data being returned in responses. For example, an application may allow the retrieval of an email address. The response should include one email address, not a list (or array) of email addresses.

For example, a JSON response containing a username and email address might look like this, which is a single object response:

```
{"username":"John",

"e-mail": "john.doe@site.com"}
```

Figure 15: A simple JSON payload encapsulating an object comprised of a username and email address

It should not look like this, which is a list of objects:

```
[ {"username":"John", "e-mail":
"john@site.com"}, {"username":"Alice", "e-
mail": "alice@site.com"} ]
```

Figure 16: A JSON payload encapsulating a list of objects

Also valuable is simply evaluating the length of the content returned, to ensure it is within an expected range. The former example, for instance, has a length of 50 characters. The latter, however, has a length of 100 characters. More data in the list would expand that length, and at some organisationally defined upper bound, should trigger a red flag.

Response length monitoring was one of the primary mitigations for Heartbleed in 2014, as the expected response was always just a few bytes, while successful exploitation of the associated vulnerability generally returned many thousand bytes.

In general, most practical implementations rely on two of the three Cs – context and content – to defend against attacks. These can be categorised more generally as inbound and outbound security.

Inbound threat mitigation

Filtering

The general rule of thumb when handling user input is to consider it tainted. 'Zero-trust' policies are beginning to be popular as a way to implement corporate wide security strategies but have long been the best defence against data-borne attacks. Trust no input that comes from a client. Whether text based or not, all input to an application should be treated as a potential attack and validated.

There are two primary approaches to filtering input: blacklisting and whitelisting.

Whitelisting compares input against a list of allowed characters and rejects those that are not on the list. Examples of whitelisting can be found virtually everywhere, as it is fairly simple to implement for numerical-only data.

Blacklisting is simpler but less effective than its counterpart. Blacklisting defines a set of known, malicious characters that, when found in input, are removed or replaced.

Filtering inbound data can be done in three logical locations in the data path:

1. On the client, when the data is being input or before submission to the app.

2. In the network, when the data is in transit. Intermediate devices, such as web application firewalls, can be used to filter data as it traverses the network.

3. In the application, when data is received. Application developers can (and should, regardless of whether it's

been filtered on the client and/or in the network) filter inbound data to ensure it is free of malicious code.

Even when all user input is validated, there still exists the potential for an attacker to evade such protections. Evasion techniques have evolved as rapidly as their protective counterparts, with a wide variety of methods used to trick even conscientious validation into letting an attack reach the data store.

Such techniques include obfuscation, through the use of alternate character sets and sophisticated escape mechanisms. Others seek out little known SQL commands that may not be included in validation checks and allow malicious input to slip through the system.

Behavioural analysis

Behavioural analysis is difficult but is increasingly of interest to security professionals as a technique to identify potential attackers in real time.

Early attempts at behavioural analysis made decisions based on static data, such as HTTP headers identifying requests as originating from bots or spiders. But some bots and spiders are desirable; for example, many application performance management systems use bots to execute transactions to gather performance metrics, and spiders are used to index sites for inclusion in search engines, such as Google and Bing.

Conversely, the identification of a client agent as a 'real' operating system and/or browser is no guarantee the transactions are legitimate. Attackers can, and do, hijack sessions and take advantage of them to execute automated transactions, or inject malicious code into the input.

Thus, behavioural analysis must go beyond static HTTP header values and examine actual behaviour against established norms for the given application and network.

One means of accomplishing this task is to use client-side scripting capabilities to inject an 'agent' which evaluates mouse movement and speed of typing to make a determination as to the humanness of the end-user. This, of course, can lead to false positive identification of 'malicious' clients, as these measurements are not able to take into account many of the factors that impact user behaviour.

Client-side agent scripting should never be taken as the deciding factor in labelling a user malicious or legitimate, but should instead be just one of the variables in a more comprehensive equation.

Behavioural analysis also includes catching logic-based attacks that attempt to skip steps in an application, or business logic flow. A typical user will branch from one step to another within a set of 'next steps'. Deviation outside those established next steps can be an indication of someone trying to circumvent expected logical flows as part of an attack. Catching these jumps outside logic requires security professionals to understand the application from a logical flow perspective. The HTTP referer header[7] (originally misspelled and never corrected)

---

[7] Referer: *http://www.site.com/page3.php*.

is an optional header that, when used, can assist security professionals and developers alike in enforcing flow and detecting anomalous behaviour.

Because this header field is optional, it is difficult to rely upon. Furthermore, the HTTP 1.1 RFC 2626 specifically requires that referers are not set when moving from HTTP to HTTPS, stating:

Clients SHOULD NOT include a Referer header field in a (non-secure) HTTP request if the referring page was transferred with a secure protocol.[8]

Within the confines of an application, however, developers can control the inclusion of the referer field and should, when possible, make sure to automatically generate this header field, so as to better enable identification of logic-based attacks.

A third means of evaluating behaviour that is particularly adept at catching denial-of-service attacks is to compare the speed at which the client sends or receives data, against their known network speed and conditions. Clients that are receiving or sending data much more slowly than their network connection is capable of, are likely throttling transmission on purpose, in order to consume more resources on the web application server and create a denial-of-service situation.

Similarly, if a client is sending requests in rapid-fire fashion, it should be considered suspect. Each page in which data must be entered takes a certain amount of time for a user to complete, and requests sent sooner than an

---

[8] *www.w3.org/Protocols/rfc2616/rfc2616.html.*

accepted 'time to fill' are likely to be an attack designed to deny service, by flooding the web application server with requests.

Signatures and anomalies

Security through signatures is a common technique. Signatures are chunks of data that, when matched, indicate the presence of malicious code. This technique is used by IPS and IDS systems to detect packet-level anomalies indicative of many types of attacks. At the application layer, signatures are used to detect a variety of attacks, including SQL injection and XSS.

Signatures are generally used by web application firewalls to detect a variety of well-known attacks. Relying solely on signatures, however, can be problematic, as it takes time to update for emerging threats, leaving systems vulnerable between discovery and defence availability.

Signatures are also vulnerable to evasion. Because signatures rely on comparisons between a specific set of characters and data, even the slightest modification of the malicious code can evade detection.

For example, many attackers will simply use URL encoding to change the look of an injection string, without changing its ultimate behaviour. Simply by changing 'NULL OR 1 = 1/*' to 'NULL+OR+1%3D1%2F%2A' is enough to bypass a signature detection system. Scanning for URL encoded characters is fraught with peril, as many applications purposefully encode data to transmit between client and server. Flagging this type of encoding as malicious could result in a high rate of false positives, frustrating users and developers alike.

Signatures used to detect established, well-known patterns is a good method of filtering out the most common and basic attacks, but like other techniques, should not be the sole source of web application security.

Client-based assistance

As noted earlier when discussing behavioural analysis, some security techniques take advantage of client-side assistance to detect potential attacks.

These are particularly helpful in detecting attacks that cannot otherwise be detected. In particular, man-in-the-browser (MITB) attacks are best detected by a client-side helper able to discern them.

MITB is not a new technique. It was first identified as a potential path to financial theft back in 2005, when Augusto Paes de Barros presented it as part of his 'The future of backdoors – worst of all worlds'. MITB didn't receive its 'official' title until it was so named in 2007 by Philipp Gühring. In 2008, Trojans with MITB capabilities began to surface: Zeus, Torpig, Clampi and Citadel.

These Trojans more often target online banking sites, with an eye towards stealing sensitive information that would allow attackers to then carry out automated transactions.

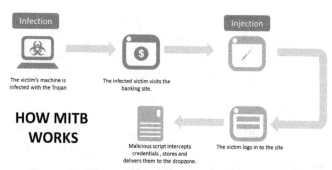

Figure 17: How man-in-the-browser attacks work

MITB attacks occur when a client is infected with a Trojan, either through an executable or a browser-based plugin. These Trojans then inject scripts and objects into a web application that are able to steal data and/or duplicate communications for the purposes of obtaining personal information.

Because of the way MITB works, client-side assistance is necessary to detect it. A client-side script can be inserted into the web application that is able to 'watch' the page. Because it knows what the original state of the application page should look like, it is able to detect any changes and notify the user.

The risk is that a user will disable the scripting necessary for the detection to occur, thus rendering it inoperable. This is true for other script-based preventative measures, such as those performing behavioural analysis. For this reason, depending solely on client-side 'agents' to detect attacks is not recommended.

On the bright side, disabling scripting also renders MITB and other script-reliant attacks inoperable.

Outbound threat mitigation

The last 'C' of web application security is content, with a focus on the outbound response. Outbound threat mitigation is the last resort; it's the last chance you have to detect an attack and prevent its successful completion.

Outbound threat mitigation cannot detect and prevent attacks designed to deny service, nor can it prevent the successful execution of an SQL injection or XSS attack. Outbound mitigation is, in almost all cases, an attempt not to stop an attack because the attack has already occurred. It is a preventive measure designed to mitigate the potential completion of the attack by preventing delivery of the 'stolen goods'.

There are two primary methods of outbound threat mitigation: data leak prevention and expectation analysis.

Both methods are generally implemented outside the web application server on an intermediary, such as a web application firewall. This is because the application itself may not have the information necessary, in all cases, to make a determination as to whether or not the data being delivered is the result of an attack or a legitimate request.

Data leak prevention

Data leak prevention is the most common means of mitigating a data exfiltration attack. Data leak prevention focuses on detecting the presence of sensitive data (as defined by the business or government regulations) and removing, or replacing it, within a response.

You've probably seen this in emails or when interacting with web applications for online banking, or any other institution with which you exchange money, 'Your account ending in: 1111' or 'Account Number: ********0001'. This indicates the presence of data leak prevention methods in action. These prevent sensitive personal and financial information from being transmitted over the network.

Data leak prevention is an outbound filtering technique, and therefore requires full access to the payload of an HTTP response, i.e. the data. Data leak prevention can be implemented by developers easily because they are in control of the data ultimately being returned by the web application.

External systems, such as proxies, load balancers and web application firewalls, are also common points in the data path to implement this mitigation. As the data flows through the system, they inspect it and scan for data matching designated patterns, such as XXX-XX-XXXX (A US Social Security Number), or an account number, such as XXX YYYY ZZZZZ, or even an email address xxxx@yyyyy.com. If the pattern is matched, its characters are changed to some other character or removed outright, and the data continues on its way.

Data leak prevention is perhaps the simplest of all mitigations to put into place, and helps prevent the most commonly targeted data – personally identifiable information.

Expectation analysis

Expectation analysis is more difficult to implement than data leak prevention but is increasingly important as a means to mitigate attacks that are more difficult to detect on the inbound stream.

Expectation analysis employs the use of expectations of content type, length, or format, and compares it to the data being received. If it differs substantially, it can be further evaluated, or rejected outright, as per the policies determined by the organisation.

Expectation analysis is particularly good at detecting a successfully executed SQL injection attack. This is because such attacks are typically executed against routines that should return only a single set of data but result in the return of multiple sets of data. By comparing the expected result, for example, one email address, against the actual results, for example 100 email addresses, systems are able to flag the response as suspicious and act according to policy.

Expectation analysis can also be used more generally to examine content type or length. If a web application typically returns a 4KB response to a URI and suddenly returns 400KB to the same URI, it's a good bet an attack has been executed. Similarly, if the object in question is an image but contains text – particularly text that appears to be a script – it is a good indication that an attack has occurred. Also valuable to examine is the payload itself. A page that deviates in structure from one response to the next may indicate a successful attack.

Applications may not be able to use this technique as readily as an external system. This has to do with the way in which most web applications are designed. Subroutines (functions) are often used to query and return data from the database, but are not provided with limitations on how many rows (data) can be returned.

Similarly, functions that rely on those subroutines may be used by other functions that might expect one row or 100. Limitations are not easily imposed on data retrieval functions that are used to retrieve varying amounts of data.

CHAPTER 5: CONCLUSION

Web application security is a stack of attack surfaces and defensive mitigating solutions. It is not enough to protect web applications with only one technique, or at only one layer of the stack. Vulnerabilities in the platform, or in protocols, such as TCP or HTTP, are just as devastating to the security and availability of applications as attacks against the application itself.

A full stack of mitigating solutions is necessary to realise a positive web application security posture. It is important to note that a comprehensive approach requires collaboration across network, security, operations and development teams, as each has a role to play in protecting applications and their critical data.

ITG RESOURCES

IT Governance Ltd sources, creates and delivers products and services to meet the real-world, evolving IT governance needs of today's organisations, directors, managers and practitioners.

The ITG website (*www.itgovernance.co.uk*) is the international one-stop-shop for corporate and IT governance information, advice, guidance, books, tools, training and consultancy. On the website you will find the following pages related to the subject matter of this book:

www.itgovernance.co.uk/iso27001.aspx

www.itgovernance.co.uk/penetration-testing.aspx.

Publishing Services

IT Governance Publishing (ITGP) is the world's leading IT-GRC publishing imprint that is wholly owned by IT Governance Ltd.

With books and tools covering all IT governance, risk and compliance frameworks, we are the publisher of choice for authors and distributors alike, producing unique and practical publications of the highest quality, in the latest formats available, which readers will find invaluable.

www.itgovernancepublishing.co.uk is the website dedicated to ITGP. Other titles published by ITGP that may be of interest include:

- Application Security in the ISO27001 Environment

  www.itgovernance.co.uk/shop/p-361.aspx

- Penetration Testing: Protecting Networks and Systems

  www.itgovernance.co.uk/shop/p-1024-penetration-testing-protecting-networks-and-systems.aspx.

We also offer a range of off-the-shelf toolkits that give comprehensive, customisable documents to help users create the specific documentation they need to properly implement a management system or standard. Written by experienced practitioners and based on the latest best practice, ITGP toolkits can save months of work for organisations working towards compliance with a given standard.

To see the full range of toolkits available please visit:

www.itgovernance.co.uk/shop/c-129-toolkits.aspx.

Books and tools published by IT Governance Publishing (ITGP) are available from all business booksellers and the following websites:

www.itgovernance.eu   *www.itgovernanceusa.com*

www.itgovernance.in   *www.itgovernancesa.co.za*

www.itgovernance.asia.

Training Services

IT Governance offers an extensive portfolio of training courses designed to educate information security, IT governance, risk management and compliance professionals. Our classroom and online training programmes will help you develop the skills required to deliver best practice and compliance to your organisation. They will also enhance your career by providing you with industry standard certifications and increased peer recognition. Our range of courses offer a structured learning path from Foundation to Advanced level in the key topics of information security, IT governance, business continuity and service management.

ISO/IEC 27001:2013 is the international management standard that helps businesses and organisations throughout the world develop a best-in-class information security management system. Knowledge and experience in implementing and maintaining ISO27001 compliance are considered to be essential to building a successful career in information security. We have the world's first programme of certificated ISO27001 education with Foundation, Lead Implementer, Risk Management and Lead Auditor training courses. Each course is designed to provide delegates with relevant knowledge and skills and an industry-recognised qualification awarded by the International Board for IT Governance Qualifications (IBITGQ).

Full details of all IT Governance training courses can be found at *www.itgovernance.co.uk/training.aspx*.

Professional Services and Consultancy

Good application security depends on regular penetration testing to determine – and mitigate – the vulnerabilities you present to the Internet.

IT Governance's consultant-driven penetration tests combine a range of advanced manual tests by our expert, CREST-accredited penetration testers with a number of automated vulnerability scans, using multiple tools and techniques, to enable you to protect your web applications from malicious attack.

Our web application penetration testing can include:

- A detailed consultation session to identify the depth and breadth of the tests required.

- Careful scoping of the test environment to establish the exact extent of the testing exercise (internal or external) dependent on your needs.

- A range of manual tests conducted by our team of highly skilled penetration testers using a methodology closely aligned with the OWASP methodology.

- A series of automated vulnerability scans.

- Immediate notification of identified critical vulnerabilities so that you can take remedial action as soon as possible.

- A detailed technical report that details the identified vulnerabilities, ranked in order of significance.

- A list of recommended countermeasures to address any identified vulnerabilities.

- An executive summary for your management team that explains in business terms what the risks mean.

IT Governance's expert consultants have over a decade's practical experience, having worked on numerous successful projects around the world with organisations of all sizes, sectors and locations, from small organisations to multinationals.

As a CREST member company, IT Governance has been verified as meeting rigorous standards of security testing. Our clients can rest assured that our technical work will be carried out by qualified and knowledgeable professionals.

For more information about penetration testing and other IT Governance technical services, please see:

www.itgovernance.co.uk/penetration-testing-packages.aspx.

Newsletter

IT governance is one of the hottest topics in business today, not least because it is also the fastest moving.

You can stay up to date with the latest developments across the whole spectrum of IT governance subject matter, including; risk management, information security, ITIL and IT service management, project governance, compliance and so much more, by subscribing to ITG's core publications and topic alert emails.

Simply visit our subscription centre and select your preferences: *www.itgovernance.co.uk/newsletter.aspx*.

EU for product safety is Stephen Evans, The Mill Enterprise Hub, Stagreenan, Drogheda, Co. Louth, A92 CD3D, Ireland. (servicecentre@itgovernance.eu)

www.ingramcontent.com/pod-product-compliance
Lightning Source LLC
LaVergne TN
LVHW052310060326
832902LV00021B/3810